foothillerg@live.com
209-368-9381

REACTIVE ROVER

AN OWNER'S GUIDE TO
ON LEASH DOG AGGRESSION:
SMALL CHANGES THAT CAN MAKE
A BIG DIFFERENCE

KIM MOELLER

Reactive Rover

An Owner's Guide to On Leash Dog Aggression:

Small Changes That Can Make A Big Difference

Kim Moeller

Kim Moeller Publishing

San Francisco, California

www.moellerdog.com

©2009 Kim Moeller

Front Cover Photo: William Hurley

Back Cover Photo: Kristine Payne

All rights reserved. No part of this book may be reproduced or transmitted in any form or by any means, electronic, digital, or mechanical, including photocopying, recording or by any information storage or retrieval system without permission in writing from the author.

Limits of Liability and Disclaimer of Warranty
The author shall not be liable in the event of incidental or consequential damages in connection with, or arising out of, the furnishing, performance, or use of the instructions and suggestions contained in this book.

ISBN 978-0-578-03379-2

DEDICATION

This book is dedicated to my chocolate Labrador Retriever, Mocha, who I had from the time she was 10 weeks old until she passed away gracefully at age 15. I owe her my dog training career. When I first got her I was an accountant. She showed me how fun training can be and how rewarding owning a dog can be. We participated in competition obedience and she earned her novice title as well as her Canine Good Citizen certificate. Yet as she got older, she started to become reactive to dogs on leash and even somewhat aggressive while off leash. So, I began to work with her on these behaviors. Over time, I switched careers to become a dog trainer, and through my experience with Mocha decided to specialize in dog aggression. Having been through this with my own dog, I completely empathize with owners who live with a dog that is aggressive, but also realize there are ways to manage and treat it successfully. And now this book gives me an opportunity to share my training tips with other owners!

ACKNOWLEDGEMENTS

Thanks to Shelley Smith for editing my book for me. I am eternally grateful to her for taking the time to put together the thoughts and ideas that I gave her for this book. Shelley graduated from the San Francisco SPCA Dog Training Academy several years ago and now teaches public dog training classes there. Shelley also provides one-on-one sessions to her private clients for all sorts of behavior issues including leash reactivity. In her "spare time," Shelley is a shelter manager for Pets Unlimited in San Francisco.

Thanks to Veronica Boutelle for her undying support in my dog training career and as my dear friend. She has given me opportunities and encouragement throughout my career and has helped me grow as an individual and as a trainer. Veronica owns and operates dogTEC, an incredible company that supports and promotes dog trainers and is the best educational support system in the world for dog trainers and pet professionals!

Thanks to William Hurley for putting up with me as a housemate, for helping me in so much of my work with this book, for producing the DVD that goes along with this book, and for many other dog projects. I could not have done it without him and he is truly a good friend!

Many, many thanks to Jean Donaldson who graciously reviewed my book and lent her expertise for some of the final editing. Jean is in no small way responsible for my dog training career. Jean gave me the opportunities at the SF/SPCA to treat dog aggression and continues to be supportive and encouraging.

Thanks to the San Francisco SPCA for giving me the opportunity to work there for the past 10 years. The SF/SPCA continues to be on the forefront of sheltering and dog training and I am proud to be affiliated with them!

Thanks to Kristine Payne for reading, rereading, and proofing the final version of this book. Her positive feedback and brainstorming gave this book its finishing touches. I am blessed by her sweet, gentle, loving, supportive self and her very handsome, fun-loving, goofy dog Samson!

AUTHOR'S NOTE

This book comes with an instructional DVD, *Reactive Rover: Managing and Training Leash Aggression*. The DVD provides a visual aid of step by step instructions on how to perform the exercises that are explained in the book. Though the book and the DVD complement each other, I recommend you read the book *first* and then watch the DVD. Having a base level of knowledge before watching the DVD will enhance your appreciation of the demos in the DVD and enable you to more effectively practice the exercises with your own dog.

I also urge all owners of reactive dogs to work with a qualified, reward-based private trainer. Through coaching, a trainer can offer spot-on insight, instill confidence, and provide feedback essential to the training process. This book is best applied when used in conjunction with a great dog trainer.

CONTENTS

INTRODUCTION

This book is designed to help owners understand and manage their dogs' reactivity on leash around other dogs. It provides a step by step practical guide to teach your dog an alternate behavior to barking on leash. If you are the owner of a reactive dog, this book should help you understand your dog's behavior while you train him to act more appropriately around other dogs. It should also provide tools to manage this behavior while you train so that your walk is a fun and positive experience rather than a stressful one.

There are many reasons why dogs are reactive to other dogs on leash. One of the most important things to remember is that your dog is not "bad" or "naughty" because he is reactive. This is a behavior that is born out of frustration or fear and occurs because your dog needs your help to change his association with other dogs from a negative one to a positive one. Dogs really do pick up cues from their handlers so this book also aims to create positive associations for you! With the right information and the best possible tools put into practice, you'll feel well-armed to take your barky best friend on walks where he will put his best paw forward.

The Honest Truths

Leash frustration can be managed and improved but rarely ever disappears 100%. Some dogs can pass by dogs with such attention to their owners that an outsider would never imagine all the hard work that has resulted in this calm focus. Other dogs will continue to need management or training everyday; there may still be some dogs who elicit reactions. This may sound daunting, but the honest truth is that there are a variety of easy techniques to help you that are dog and owner friendly, and they are here in this book!

Here are a few more truths you must consider. These are minor changes to your daily life that will provide immediate relief as well as pave the way for your new training plan.

#1 Practice Situational Awareness

This fancy term really means that you are always aware of your surroundings and focused on being a team with your dog. It means driving defensively when walking your dog. You must constantly be looking in front of you, behind you and to the sides of you, watching for oncoming "traffic." This may sound stressful or hard to do, and it can take some getting used to. But imagine when you drive an actual car down the road; defensive drivers drive well without even thinking about it. This same second-nature skill will be yours when you have put new techniques into practice on a regular basis.

#2 Every Walk Is A "Training Moment"

This means you always get to wear your "dog trainer hat" when out with your dog. You'll now always be prepared for a training moment with tasty treats and happy talk and a new arsenal of techniques and tools. Be ready to drink your coffee before the walk, not during, and put your cell phone on silent! This time belongs to you and your dog, and you can now feel prepared to be proactive rather than reactive, which simply means that things will go much better if you get your dog's attention and focus *before* he starts to bark and pull. You have probably already noticed that is it much harder to get your dog's focus and attention back on you once he is barking and lunging, so from now on your defensive driving will prevent this.

#3 Be Your Dog's Best Friend...After All, You're His

Finally, remember to enjoy your dog. You'll soon be learning and growing with him which is a very exciting and rewarding experience. You'll get to watch firsthand as he begins to react positively to the same dogs that previously sent him over the edge. This is an amazing transition to watch.

If you've been having rough times with your dog, vow to make a fresh start. It can help enormously to remind yourself not to take things too seriously. For instance, try this trick next time you go out for a walk: dress your dog up in something cute like a t-shirt or sweater, a cute bandana, bells around his neck, or a cute hat and see the different response people give you if your dog reacts. They will have a harder time taking your dog seriously when your dog looks cute and silly, and so will you. I bet you smile at least twice!

Now, before you turn the page and get more into this book, go hug your dog and tell him you just committed to a new plan that promises to be fun for both of you. Tell him you love him. I bet you he gives you a tail wag back. Then, pick up the book again and get started!

Chapter 1

Reasons for Leash Reactivity

Why does my dog act like this?

Y ou may wonder why your dog acts like a monster on leash and your neighbor's dog doesn't, or why your dog changes from exploding beast to perfect park playmate as soon as the leash comes off. There are several different possibilities that can be sorted into three rough categories.

The Hyper-Motivated Dog

This dog is likely to bark and strain on leash because he is excited to approach and meet another dog but frustrated because he can't do it *right now*. This frustration can lead to a high state of arousal (the dog trainer's term for emotional excitement) and he may bark or lunge to vent this. Hyper-motivated dogs often show appropriate greeting behaviors once they get to actually meet another dog (if they haven't scared them away with their fireworks display!) These dogs almost always enjoy playing with other dogs when the leash is off.

Previous Aversive Training Experiences

Another reason dogs bark and lunge at other dogs is that they have developed a bad association between seeing another dog and getting punished by the handler, usually with an aversive training device like a prong or choke collar. Choke collars, pinch or prong collars, and shock collars are designed to stop dogs from barking at other dogs by causing pain. The best case scenario when one of these tools is used is that the handler correctly times the correction so that the dog is actually punished for pulling or barking. Although the dog might stop barking because the correction hurts, this doesn't change the dog's feelings about other dogs, and can even cause the dog to ultimately dislike dogs. This is because punishment – even if well-timed – delivers pain when another dog approaches. At the most basic level of the dog's psyche is this: dogs predict pain. Many dogs may then become *more* aggressive on leash in hopes of making the other dog go away so that pain is avoided.

Undersocialized Or Fearful Dogs

Some dogs are afraid of being approached by other dogs, often due to a lack of socialization or exposure. For example, many backyard dogs are leash reactive because they missed out on encountering other dogs often enough. They either don't learn proper dog manners at all, or are rough around the edges from infrequent interactions. Very often they become fearful of other dogs. They may bark to make the other dog increase his distance, that is, to make them go away. From the dog's perspective, even if things unfold normally in a pass-by situation, his display works because the other dog does indeed continue on. Dogs never fail to do what works for them, so it's very likely they'll bark again, maybe louder, maybe sooner, next time.

Dogs can also become fearful of other dogs because of a bad experience. Being attacked can be traumatic for any dog, especially puppies who are so impressionable. While most dogs will not have lasting negative effects from an incident, some young or sensitive dogs, or dogs experiencing a particularly scary event may need help to feel comfortable again.

Fearful or undersocialized dogs would probably choose to avoid approaching dogs but cannot because they are on leash. Forcing these uncomfortable dogs to interact repeatedly with dogs may exacerbate their aggressive behavior. If you suspect your dog is fearful of other dogs, be especially protective of him. Never force him to interact with other dogs, and avoid letting dogs overwhelm him by rushing up to him, even if they appear friendly. Pay special attention to *Chapter 4: Thresholds*.

A sub-category of undersocialization includes asocial dogs and dogs who are proximity sensitive to other dogs. These are dogs who, while not frankly fearful, have no interest in playing or sometimes even interacting with other dogs. Dogs who are proximity sensitive are sensitive to dogs "in their personal bubbles," or "in their space." Often they show no reactions until dogs get too close, and then may growl, snarl, or snap to get the other dog to increase their distance.

Most dogs grow increasingly asocial or selective of playmates as they mature. This is completely normal, and commonly occurs between one and three years of age. This is especially true of adult females. Some snapping or growling is almost to be expected, and shouldn't be considered a problem necessarily, unless the dog is repeatedly doing damage to other dogs (such as punctures that require sutures).

These categories are not hard and fast, and often dogs will have components of more than one. For example, an undersocialized backyard dog may also be hyper-motivated to approach and greet dogs. What's perhaps most fabulous about using positive reinforcement on your reactive dog is that no matter what the reason, you are likely to achieve a change in behavior.

CHAPTER 2

TRAINING TOOLS

WHAT YOU'LL NEED TO BEGIN HELPING YOUR DOG

Let's talk about a few new tools that you will need to begin helping your dog. You will find that having the proper equipment when walking reactive Rover, arming yourself with special yummy treats, and learning how to communicate effectively to your dog will be extremely helpful. Let's learn more.

Walking Equipment: Power Steering For Your Reactive Dog

You may already be using one of the helpful new harnesses or head collars on the market. If not, you will want to look into the best option for your dog. If you are using a prong collar or choke collar, investing in alternate equipment is a must for this program.

Gentle Leaders and *Haltis* are head collars. These work like halters for horses. You wouldn't expect to direct or control a five hundred pound horse by looping its neck; instead, you get control of the head. Where the head goes, the body follows, and Gentle Leaders and Haltis help you gently move your dog where you want them.

Most dogs are not used to walking with something on their face, so some time is needed to help the dog adjust. A simple plan for head collar desensitization can be found online at www.gentleleader.com. It's a little extra work, but well worth it!

SENSE-ible Harnesses are similar to traditional body harnesses with one small important twist: their design discourages pulling instead of encouraging it! These harnesses go on like traditional ones, but the leash clips to the chest to help you direct your dog. The trade-off with this choice of equipment is that you get less power steering than with the head collars, but most dogs acclimate to these immediately, so no need for desensitization. More information on this great harness can be found online at www.softouchconcepts.com.

Training Ammunition And Where To Carry It

Now that you've chosen to change your dog's association with other dogs, you'll need to carry secret stashes of your dog's favorite training treats. Especially in the beginning stages of training, these should be extra yummy, super smelly, and new or different. Tiny pieces of chopped steak, chicken, turkey, and cheese are great, as well as baby food right from the jar. Macaroni and cheese (pre-sized, no chopping needed!), freeze dried liver, and meatballs chopped up work well too. Make a week's worth of treats, pop them into plastic bags, and freeze them. Then, you'll be ready for walks and training sessions with no more work involved. Ammunition prep is a habit well worth cultivating.

You'll want to keep your training food in an easily accessible location while on walks. A jacket pocket or sweatshirt pouch can work great, or you can invest in a bait pouch or treat bag specifically for training. These usually hook on your belt or clip around your waist, and snap open and closed for easy to reach treats.

Good Communication: A Marker Word

We don't often think about it, but dogs don't communicate verbally like we do. When they seem to know the meaning of words it's because they've learned to associate the particular word with something that happens to them. Think of your dog's reaction when you say "Walkies" or "Are you hungry?" They know these words are usually followed by a fun walk or good food. In order for your dog to know right away that their improved behavior has won them a treat, you'll need to mark his behavior with a special word. When your dog sits, or looks at another dog without barking or staring, mark the behavior with your special word, then reward. You're using precision communication to tell your dog what you like so he'll do more of it. Choose any word you like, provided you don't use it often in everyday conversation. You really want your dog to have a strong association with it: Marker word = treats. Be creative – this is like a secret code word for your dog. Some great markers I've heard clients use are "Yes," "Score," "Good," "Bingo," and "Snap."

To teach the association, grab a handful of treats. Say the word, take a breath, then feed or toss the treat to your dog. Make sure not to speak and toss simultaneously. Wait a bit, then do it again. After a few handfuls, your dog should look at you or at the source of your treats when you say the word – job well done! You're almost ready to go "on the road!"

CHAPTER 3

A FEW NEW RULES

Little changes in your dog's everyday routine can make a big difference in modifying reactive behavior. Increasing your dog's aerobic exercise to one hour per day is a fantastic start. Walks are great but don't always get a dog's heart rate pounding, so make time for Frisbee, fetch, tug, or beach runs each day. If your dog plays well with others off-leash, increase his dog play time to really saturate him with fun dog experiences and get him worn out and tired. If he's just spent 45 minutes romping with Merlin, Stevie, and Bug, he won't be as hyper if he has to pass by Willie on leash on the way home.

In addition to physical exercise, mental stimulation is invaluable as well. Feeding your dog in work-to-eat or puzzle toys alleviates boredom and is plain fun. You can absolutely go all the way and feed *exclusively* in toys like Kongs, Dogzillas, Tricky Treat Balls, and Tug a Jugs to keep your dog happily occupied while you're at work or on the computer.

Nothing In Life Is Free—And We're *Really* Happy About It!

Dogs are working animals. When you think about it, dogs in natural environments would work for everything they get, but since we've stepped in, we've handed them everything on a bone-shaped silver platter. Your dog will be mentally healthier and happier, as well as physically calmer and better mannered, if you ask him to work in order to access his favorite things. This includes food and treats, of course, but also walks, toys, passage in and out of the car and house, petting and affection from you, and so on. Your dog will also learn to listen more closely and pay greater attention to you, since you are now the giver of all good things. He now needs to go through you for anything he needs!

This program is as simple as asking for a "Sit" or a "Down" before putting the food bowl down or putting the leash on. Ask your dog to show off his trick repertoire before meeting a new person, or before he gets his breakfast Kong. Teach your dog to "Wait" or "Stay" before you let them through doors. This not only keeps him working, but also is very polite behavior and a safe practice: no rushing into the hallway or street without knowing what's coming. This pause before exiting habit is important so do it every time: step through first and make sure the environment is right before your dog dashes into it.

"Happy Talk:" Using Your Cookie Voice To Your Advantage

Devoting a paragraph to giggling may seem strange for a book on leash reactivity, but it's an integral part of a successful plan. Think about the way your dog reacts when you laugh at something he's done, or when you ask him in a high-pitched "talking-to-the-dog" voice if he wants cookies. He lights up! Tail wags, ears go forward, tongue may come out, and wiggling—all these mean your dog has a very positive emotional response to your cookie voice. They already have this, so you may as well put it in your training toolbox.

When your dog sees another dog, act silly, giggle, or use your cookie voice. For instance, as soon as a dog appears within sight of your dog, instantly giggle and say in your "want a cookie" voice, "Oooh! There's your best friend the big crazy dog, look there he is!" Your dog will look at you like you're crazy the first time, but guess what—if he's looking at you, he's not barking! Well done. Now reward that.

One other important reason to use the cookie voice or giggle routine is that it changes the way *you* react to the sight of another dog too. Very few people can pull up on the leash, get tense, and go "Eeeeeeeiiiiiii!" if they are giggling and saying "Oh fabulous! Your favorite dog Cujo is coming down the street. Let's duck behind this car, heehee!" Try it if you don't believe me. And, if you are concerned about what your neighbors will think of you giggling on the street, they'll probably think, "Wow, what a difference, I thought that dog used to bark and lunge at my dog. The owner sure seems happy about the change too!"

CHAPTER 4

THRESHOLDS

From this point on, you'll be keeping your dog "under *threshold*" at all times. Your dog's threshold is the point at which he exhibits his reactive behavior. You'll need to time your intervention moment so it occurs in the time envelope between your dog *seeing* another dog and his *reaction* to that dog. For example, let's say your dog sees another dog thirty feet away, but doesn't bark or pull until the dog is twenty feet away. You'll start training at thirty feet. In fact, you'll only attempt training at twenty-five feet when your dog performs well at thirty feet. And only when he performs well at twenty-five feet will you attempt the previously problematic twenty foot distance.

You might ask why it's necessary to wait until your dog sees the other dog to commence training. Why not try to be vigilant and start training before he sees the dog? The answer is that in order for training to take place, the other dog must be the predictor of all this good stuff happening. But because being too close will elicit a reaction from your dog that is detrimental to the training cause, you are always striving for the "goldilocks zone": that split second between seeing another dog and reacting to that dog. Here's a human example to illustrate staying under threshold. If you were afraid of monkeys, and someone was trying to teach you that monkeys predict good things, you wouldn't learn this if you kept getting bombarded by monkeys at close range. In fact, you may become more worried, as you won't know when one will appear or how close.

You can keep your dog successfully under his threshold by juggling the **Three D's of Training**: Distance, Duration, and Distraction. Determining distance involves noticing how far away your dog is from another dog when he alerts to her, and how far away when he barks or lunges. This will give you your "goldilocks" range. In the example above, your dog has a ten-foot working range (between thirty and twenty feet). If you miss it and get too close and your dog goes off, you need to do a management technique like Find It or a Turn and Go (discussed in greater detail in *Chapter 5: Management Strategies for Leash Reactivity*). So, the rule is: your training moment occurs in the space after he notices the dog but before he goes off.

Duration refers to how long your dog is in the presence of another dog, whether it's while passing one on the street or making eye contact. Many dogs can look briefly at another dog but will bark or growl if allowed to stare for longer than a few seconds. Prompting or luring a watch-the-trainer is a great way to decrease the time your dog spends looking at another dog, because he must look away and back to you to get rewarded.

Because of the necessity of properly managing duration, most dogs new to training will need the *two-second rule*: they can look at another dog for two seconds, but if they haven't looked back at you by then, they need to be prompted with a verbal cue, some happy talk, or a lure, to look away. This great rule of thumb will also help build your Auto-Watch, so further down the line even if you fail to prompt, your dog will shift focus back to you after two seconds. Another way to manipulate duration is to move quickly past dogs you encounter. As you progress in training, you will slow down to a regular walking pace. So, while at first you may have to race by another dog while singing a happy tune at the top of your lungs, later you can work your dog up to amazing Auto-Watches or an extended Watch while you walk by calmly with minimal cheerleading. Watch and Auto-Watch are discussed in greater detail in *Chapter 6: Teaching Alternative Behaviors*.

Finally, Distraction is the third *D* you'll be juggling while you train, and this refers to what competing motivators exist for your dog in a given situation. Are there multiple dogs nearby, or just one? Is there construction going on nearby, or people picnicking with running kids and fried chicken? Interestingly, while to us these are distractions from our training plan, to your dog, they are actually the primary motivators if they are more attractive than what you are offering: in other words, to your dog *you* are the distraction at that moment! He wants to meet another dog or get some coleslaw, and here you are asking him to watch you or sit at the curb! This means you'll have to upgrade your motivators (happy talk, better treats, pull out the tug toy, etc.) as well as make the other two *D*'s easier—this is the juggling act of successful training. If Distractions are high, create more Distance and move by as quickly as possible to minimize Duration. For instance, if you spot a dog walker with three Bichons all barking on leash themselves, a good way to juggle is to cross the street or duck behind a parked car to increase distance and break your dog's visual connection. Perhaps you'll also want to bring out the summer sausage instead of the dried liver bits to help trump those yappy pups!

Put your Three D juggling into use whenever you need to adjust your training or management scenario in order for your dog to be successful at giving you his attention and not going off at a dog. This will keep your dog under his threshold and more able to use his thinking brain than his reacting brain. For most dogs, you can be fairly certain they are at a comfortable distance for training if they can take treats from you gently, perform an easy behavior you ask of them, and are not barking, growling, or pulling on the leash. If your dog is not taking treats you offer or isn't listening to you, he is too upset to think and you need to make it easier for your dog using your Three D's.

CHAPTER 5

MANAGEMENT STRATEGIES FOR LEASH REACTIVITY

Management techniques prevent the problem, are easy to implement and require little or no training to be successful. They help keep your dog under threshold when you're just out on a walk, rather than training per se, and need to just pass a dog without drama. Sometimes it's just not a good time to train and sometimes you just don't feel like training. *Management* to the rescue.

The "Find It" Game

This is the easiest exercise to do with a reactive dog, especially when you are new to training. Dogs learn it quickly, and you can always fall back on it should you find yourself in a tough situation. On your next walk, grab a handful of tasty treats and head out. Say "Find It" and toss a treat onto the ground just ahead of your dog. When he drops his head to look for it, say "Find It" again and toss another. Your goal is to keep your dog searching for the food on the ground for several feet. Practice until your dog immediately looks to the ground when you say "Find It." Now when you see a dog ahead of you that you must pass, immediately say "Find It" and toss treats quickly, keeping your dog's head and eyes low on the ground rather than staring at the dog. During the actual pass, toss the treat out *in front and away* from the other dog to help redirect your dog's body and focus. You may need to give a wide distance in the beginning even with the Find It game, but doing this greatly decreases opportunity for reactivity.

Body Blocking

One of the best ways to manage reactivity is to prevent your dog from seeing another dog, and if he does see one, to prevent him from staring at the other dog. I recommend the *two-second rule*. If your dog sees another dog, avoid any looking or staring for more than two seconds. You can do this by stepping on the other side of a car, turning a corner, or crossing the street. If you get caught without one of these environmental blocks, use your body to create a visual barrier. Step into the space in front of your dog as close to him as you can—the bigger you are the more visual space you'll block. The point is not to lean over him or be intimidating, but rather to cleanly step into his space to shift his focus from the dog to you. Once he is looking at you, say your marker word (like "Yes!") and feed him a treat. Continue to feed and happy talk your dog until the other dog is gone. Remember, this is management technique, so you aren't trying to train your dog at this time, just get him past the other dog without rehearsing any reactive behavior.

Turn-and-Go

The Turn-and-Go exercise is just as it sounds: when you see another dog (hopefully before your dog does, as this is management) you turn around in the opposite direction and walk briskly away, keeping your dog's focus on you. Think of it as a "get out of Dodge" exercise! For the smoothest execution, say your dog's name in a happy voice, then turn *away from* your dog in the other direction and keep moving and happy talking until you are out of sight of the other dog or at a distance appropriate to do some training. If you walk your dog on your left side, turn to the right when you see the other dog. If you walk your dog on your right, turn to the left to make your retreat. Keep the dog moving no matter what; even if your dog sees the other dog, and even if he begins reacting, you're still going to go quickly in the opposite direction, and if possible get a Watch or Hand Target from your dog (discussed in greater detail in *Chapter 6: Teaching Alternative Behaviors*). If you can't get a Watch or Hand Target, play the Find It game until you are at a manageable distance.

Back-Up Recall

The Back-Up Recall is similar to the Turn-and-Go because it is a distance-increasing exercise. However, with the Back-Up Recall, you will back up quickly on the street with your dog facing you instead of you both going in the same direction. It is really a "come when I call you" exercise but amid a high level of distraction. This technique is helpful for a variety of reasons. If you need to lure or feed your dog to keep his attention on you, his nose is right there for you to control while you are backing up to create more distance. It's also great because as you increase distance, you can monitor the other dog to know what he and his handler are doing; are they crossing the street, getting into a car, or following your path? This information can help you adjust your trajectory. You can also do a Back-Up Recall for several feet, get your dog into a sit and use the time this has bought you to let the other dog pass or do some training if you decide it might be a training opportunity. To practice the Back-Up Recall, when you see another dog, quickly say "Roofus, Come!" and then begin backing up. Your dog should look to you and then move toward you (the recall part) and you can either feed, lure, or ask for a Sit or Watch. Practice this in a quiet area the first several times until your dog immediately looks at you and moves toward you when you call him.

An important part to remember when using the Turn-and-Go and the Back-Up Recall is that the leash never has to go taut during these exercises. You are using other tools to control, direct, and focus your dog. Tools like your voice, body language, movement, and food are much more positive and easy to use than a tight leash. Remember that a tight leash can encourage or exacerbate reactivity, so avoid it if at all possible.

CHAPTER 6

TEACHING

ALTERNATIVE

BEHAVIORS

Once you've learned to manage your dog on leash to avoid altercations and less than flattering displays, you are ready to train your dog to do something other than bark or growl when he sees a dog. You will teach him simple behaviors he can do that are incompatible with barking, lunging, growling, or staring. The simplest alternative behaviors are **Watch**, **Hand Targeting**, and **Leave It**.

"Watch"

Training your dog to Watch simply means training him to look into your face or eyes when you ask. Once it's taught, your dog will look into your eyes instead of barking or lunging.

To begin teaching Watch, grab a handful of tiny treats or your dog's kibble and find a quiet place in your home. Say "Roofus (use your dog's name), Watch" in a happy tone. When he looks at you, say your marker word (like "Yes!") and feed him a treat. Repeat this until he looks at you immediately after you say "Watch." Then, begin to delay saying "Yes!" for a second or two, until he maintains focus on you for longer durations. If he does not look up towards you, continue your happy talk to get his attention. If he still does not look at you even for a second, put a tiny treat in your hand and hold it right in front of his nose, so close it's like Velcro. Then draw a line with your treat from his nose to your eyes. He should follow the treat right up to your face; when he does, say "Yes!" and give him the food. Do this same luring technique five times, saying "Yes!" and feeding him each time, then try it with an empty hand making the same motion as when you had food. This will become your Watch hand signal if you need it.

Once he can Watch you every time you ask for it, begin to add distractions. Work the exercise outside or in a busier area (avoid dogs until you've added all other distractions). Enlist a friend's help by having her hold a toy or a treat at a distance and then asking your dog to Watch. Once your dog is fluent at this, begin working while on walks, but in areas where you are not likely to see dogs. When your dog Watches immediately on these walks, you are ready to try it with dogs at a distance. You want your dog to have practiced so much it will seem like muscle memory to him. While your Watch is in training, use your Turn-and-Go, Back-Up Recall, or Find Its for dog encounters.

If you are in a distracting environment and luring doesn't work, use a Body Block—step in front of him very close to block his view and then ask for a Watch or lure one. Being the biggest thing in his view can really help him focus on you.

Your ultimate goal with this piece of training is to develop an **Auto-Watch**. With enough practice your dog will see another dog and look at you on his own. Remember to protect your Auto-Watch by not trying to progress too quickly in the training process. Decrease distance to dogs gradually and steadily for the best results.

Hand Targeting, Or "Touch"

Hand Targeting is super easy for you and your dog – all you teach your dog to do is touch his nose to the palm of your hand. To begin, have some small treats ready and bring your dog to a quiet area. The first time you offer your hand, your dog will likely investigate it, which gives you an instant correct response, so be ready with your marker word (like "Yes!") – don't miss that first opportunity! Put your empty hand in front of your dog, close enough that they can easily sniff it but without doing the actual touch (this is his part of the work). As soon as your dog puts his nose on your palm, say your marker word (like "Yes!") and then treat. Don't worry about saying anything yet to cue him to do this – train silently if possible. Repeat until your dog immediately noses your hand when it's presented to him, then begin making it a little harder by moving your hand farther away so he must stretch out or take a step in order to hit the hand target.

As he becomes proficient (you'll know because he won't delay any more when you put your hand down), experiment to see how far he'll follow your hand. Will he take two steps? Three? When he does a few steps consistently you can add the command by saying "Touch" or "Target" *before* you present your hand. Once the cue is added, the next step is to add distractions. Work on a quiet street, then slowly up to having dogs enter the scene. Cue the target, present your hand, and reward for nose touches!

"Leave It"

Leave It is another focus exercise for your dog. Once trained, your dog should turn his head away from the distraction (food, garbage, person, dog, etc) and physically orient himself toward you. Are you beginning to see a pattern here? We want to reward our dogs for looking to us instead of acting on impulses. If they are focused on us, they are too busy to bark at dogs!

As usual, we begin with a very easy exercise and graduate to harder levels as your dog is successful. The baby step Leave It involves just learning to come off food in your hand. Start with a boring treat like kibble or a dry biscuit. Close your hand around it and present it to your dog. Tell him "Leave It" – one time only – and then wait him out. He will probably lick, nibble, or nudge your hand. Some dogs may try for quite some time before pausing. As soon as your dog hesitates, say your marker word and reward your dog with a really good treat from your other hand. Repeat several times; you should notice your dog takes less time to stop nibbling and nudging. Your goal is to say "Leave It" and have your dog look away from the food. It's even better if he looks toward your other hand or up to your face. Remember to say "Leave It" only once—you want your dog to know you want immediate results, not after you've said "Leave It" four or five times.

Leave It at the next level involves treats on the ground. As with the baby Leave It, use boring treats for leaving and great ones for rewarding. The key to this step is making sure your dog never beats you to the treat on the floor, or else he will learn "Leave It" doesn't mean much. For insurance, ask someone to help you by standing close by to protect the Leave It treat, or put a clear, sturdy bowl or cup over the treat. A leash can also provide a line of defense against grabbing in this exercise. Practice walking your dog past the food (remember you can manipulate your dog's distance from the food to make it easier or harder), and *when you see your dog look at the food*, say "Leave It." If your dog looks away from the food or looks at you, say your marker word, cheerlead him for his great choice and immediately furnish the better treat stashed in your pouch! If your dog doesn't look away, put your good treat right on his nose and lure his attention to you. Reward when you've got it. Regardless of what the dog does, keep walking! It's easy to get excited that your dog got it right, and get stuck luring and standing, but resist this temptation and keep moving. This avoids the dog that Leaves It, gets rewarded, and goes right back to the distraction! Also, avoid using the leash to pull your dog away from the food as much as possible – use your tools instead: good treats, happy talk, and moving away with your own body. Practice this until your dog refocuses on you automatically when you say "Leave It."

When he's good at it, now you can begin to use Leave It for many different distractions. Try a toy, ball, or familiar person. Remember each time you introduce a new distraction, you'll have to make the exercise a little easier (such as with greater distance) until your dog learns the same rules apply. Finally, you can begin to use Leave It with dogs at a distance. When trained well, this is a great emergency command if you're surprised by an off-leash dog.

CONCLUSION

Dogs, like us, have good and bad days. During training and beyond, don't stress if your dog has a bad day, the next one will be better. If it helps, keep a journal to chart his progress. You'll be able to recognize small changes and stay focused on the big picture. Always keep your dog under threshold and stay positive. You're already one step closer having read this book. You are that extraordinary person who wants your dog to have the best manners and be the happiest he can be! You know you're committed to your dog, so now, close the book, go give your dog a hug and tell him things are going to be fun and enjoyable now for both of you! Grab your treats, get focused, and get started. With your "game plan" in mind as you head out the door, you and your dog will be able to handle almost anything!